THEN & NOW®

GRAND HAVEN

Opposite: This 1868 photograph, taken from Dewey Hill, reveals a small town of about 3,000 people. The buildings at the foot of the dune were constructed because the railroad depot was located there. Passengers were transported to Grand Haven on ferryboats. None of the major buildings appearing in the photograph exist today on either side of the Grand River. (Wallace K. Ewing.)

THEN & NOW®

GRAND HAVEN

Wallace K. Ewing, Ph.D.,
and Elizabeth Dobbie for the
Tri-Cities Historical Museum

ISBN 978-0-7385-7706-7

Library of Congress Control Number: 2009925636

Published by Arcadia Publishing
Charleston, South Carolina

Printed in the United States of America

For all general information contact Arcadia Publishing at:
Telephone 843-853-2070
Fax 843-853-0044
E-mail sales@arcadiapublishing.com
For customer service and orders:
Toll-Free 1-888-313-2665

Visit us on the Internet at www.arcadiapublishing.com

On the front cover: In 1900, the Story and Clark Piano Company of Chicago was secured by the board of trade as the first large industrial addition to the city of Grand Haven. Construction of the factory began in December of that year, and production started in 1901. In 1905, the three-story brick structure, shown here, was erected on the west side of North First Street between Washington and Columbus Streets adjacent to the first building. It has been converted to retail shops, a restaurant, and condominiums. (Historic image, Tri-Center Historical Museum; contemporary image, Elizabeth Dobbie.)

On the back cover: In 1871, the Spring Lake Magnetic Mineral Spring Company constructed a $70,000 hotel that consisted of a four-story main building with 74 rooms plus four eight-room cottages with a total of 30 rooms. In an 1893 brochure, the management claimed, "The Bethlehem Mineral Springs, owned by the Hotel Company possess qualities of rare merit and some wonderful cures have been effected by their use, and are specially adapted to disorders of the Stomach, Liver, Kidneys, Eczema, etc." (Wallace K. Ewing.)

Contents

Acknowledgments		7
Introduction		9
1.	Along the Lakes and River	11
2.	Estates, Homes, and Cottages	29
3.	Travel by Train, Boat, and Car	41
4.	Churches, Schools, and Libraries	53
5.	Public and Private Places	71
6.	Commercial and Manufacturing Sites	81

Acknowledgments

This book differs from the first three published by Arcadia on the Grand Haven area in that the historic images are supplemented by photographs of buildings and sites as they appear today. The picture postcards from Wallace K. Ewing's collection provided most of the historic images. Elizabeth Dobbie supplied the contemporary photographs. As with the other books, the Tri-Cities Historical Museum, Loutit District Library, and the *Grand Haven Tribune* contributed to the project. We also thank Bruce Baker for lending us a rare archival photograph of Baker Lumber. Our community is blessed with an abundance of archives and artifacts that document its rich history, and it is further blessed with residents and visitors who are fascinated with the area's early years. Over many decades, the museum, library, and newspaper have willingly taken on the challenge of recording and storing historical information that is easily accessed by historians and citizens curious about their roots.

Finally the authors extend congratulations to the city of Grand Haven, which on November 2, 2009, celebrated its 175th anniversary. We appreciate the opportunity to be a part of the celebration by publishing this volume in the Then & Now series.

INTRODUCTION

When American pioneers pressed westward in the early 1800s, they avoided Michigan like the plague. Perhaps they preferred other territories because they did indeed fear a plague, malaria, or some other insect-borne disease in Michigan. The "Wolverine State" had a reputation as a place consisting of marshes, swamps, and low-lying land swarming with mosquitoes. Despite that reputation, the opening of the Erie Canal in 1825 made the journey to Michigan easier. Boarding boats in Buffalo, settlers could sail west on Lake Erie, north on Lake Huron, and down Lake Michigan to any number of ports. Grand Haven offered one of the best ports on the big lake, a convenience that helped offset the nuisance of flying insects. In addition, Michigan's longest river, the Grand, emptied into Lake Michigan at Grand Haven's harbor. About a mile from the mouth of the Grand River, a body of water the Native Americans called the "Big Bayou" provided another attraction. Today that bayou is called Spring Lake. The first settlers, under the leadership of Rev. William M. Ferry, arrived on Sunday, November 2. Some of Ferry's party stayed aboard ship that winter; others bedded down in a fur-trading post run by Rix Robinson. By the next fall, permanent homes had been built, warehouses constructed, and the first sawmill was in operation. By the middle of the 19th century, railroads made the migration to Grand Haven even easier.

In short time, a dozen or so sawmills were built along the Grand River, some in the village of Ferrysburg, just over the river from Grand Haven, and others in the village of Spring Lake, a little east of Ferrysburg. With the growth of America and an ever-increasing demand for lumber, the communities thrived and the population multiplied. However, what had seemed like an endless supply of lumber turned out to be finite, and by 1890, the lumberjacks had moved west. With them went the economy. Business leaders who remained behind conferred and organized a board of trade that attracted manufacturing businesses, some wood-related and others more diverse.

Meanwhile, a new industry was taking hold: tourism. The Lake Michigan waterfront, the Grand River, and the adjacent Spring Lake made the area a perfect water wonderland for vacationers, who started arriving as early as 1870 when magnetic mineral springs were discovered beneath the sandy surface. These magical springs encouraged the development of large resort hotels, whose aim was to attract and then spoil visitors with comfortable living quarters and hearty food and bracing air. A growing middle class from big cities throughout the Midwest, such as St. Louis and Chicago, discovered a paradise of cool lake breezes, expansive sandy beaches, and excellent fishing here. Visitors came by the trainload and the boatload in the late 1800s and into the 20th century. The Tri-Cities thrived once again.

Manufacturing and tourism infused the area with new money that helped build highways and streets, homes and shops, factories, resorts, and cottages. The images in this book show those early structures and sites in photographs and picture postcards that vacationers enjoyed sending to family and friends. "Having a wonderful time, wish you were here," was the essence of most messages. Photographs of the same sites today convey the extent to which the community has changed or has remained the same.

Change is inevitable. Yesterday's manufacturing economy has diminished, replaced in large part by a growing variety of retail shops and services. Many changes were subtle, taking place over long periods of time; others were fast and dramatic. Yet the overall effect of these changes was extensive and intensive. During the area's various periods of growth and decline, Grand Haven, Spring Lake, Ferrysburg, and the surrounding townships have survived remarkably well. Although no one world famous was born or lived here, several citizens nudged the perimeter of fame or notoriety. Through it all, the area has retained its small-town look and feel and its devotion to family, to country, and to God. Fifty years from now, inquisitive historians will see the contemporary images as quaint relics of the past, deserving of a new Then & Now volume.

CHAPTER 1

ALONG THE LAKES AND RIVER

Fishing for perch on the south pier has long been an outdoor activity for nimrods of all ages, but sophisticated rods and reels have largely replaced yesterday's cane poles and live bait. The change in equipment has not lessened the thrill of the catch.

In 1855, the government built high on Five Mile Hill the second lighthouse to guide ships into Grand Haven harbor. The tower, shown in this pre-1907 postcard view, stood 150 feet above lake level, and its light could be seen 25 miles out. In 1910, the tower was removed and the living quarters were expanded. The renovated structure served as a residence for the lighthouse keeper and his family until 1939. The building was sold in 1956 and converted to privately owned residential property.

This early-1900s view of the south pier in rough weather reveals the wood planks, posts, and beams that were used in its original construction. Today slabs of concrete provide a stable walking surface, and the catwalk, no longer used, is constructed of steel. The pier makes an ideal promenade for anyone wishing to see the sunset over Lake Michigan.

Formerly the property of the U.S. Coast Guard, the two-story frame dormitory building and four-stall boathouse located across the channel and unused by the guard since 1989 was bought by a private party that remodeled the larger structure into a residence in the early 1990s. The Coast Guard station shown in the postcard was built in 1922. The original two-stall marine garage was expanded to four stalls in 1937.

Government Pond, also known as Government Basin, was formed in 1857 when revetments were installed to stop erosion caused by the Grand River's currents and to improve the channel for boats. The pond is kept deep enough to moor vessels of various sizes. In 1989, the Coast Guard moved from its 1922 building on the north side of the channel to a new building on Government Pond, as seen in the contemporary picture.

In 1920, Grand Haven turned over 22 acres of Lake Michigan property to the State of Michigan for $1. The next year, an oval-shaped 25-foot-wide strip of concrete was laid in the state park to allow easier motoring and to provide space for parking. The shape of the concrete circuit inspired people to refer to the area as the "Oval." Land was added over the years, especially to the east, bringing the total holdings to more than 44 acres.

In the mid-1930s, the American Legion ran a canteen at the Oval, offering sandwiches, popcorn, candy, cigars, cigarettes, soft drinks, and ice cream. In 1938, a brick pavilion near the center of the Oval replaced the earlier frame structure. In the late 1930s or early 1940s, another concession was built at the north end of the park, where bait and refreshments were sold. The pavilion today looks essentially the same as when it was built.

Today's Bil-Mar Restaurant, the building in the foreground, was the site of August Boseker's pavilion. Erected in 1898, it underwent numerous changes over the years before ending up as a restaurant. In 1907, Boseker purchased the Munroe interurban station near the site of today's campgrounds in the state park and moved it to a spot just north of Boseker's Pavilion. There it became a dance hall known as Hyland Gardens, the three-story building in the background. Today Lighthouse Condominiums occupies the site.

In 1921, Ed Peters enlarged Hyland Gardens and put in a skating rink, bathhouses, and other facilities in the large frame structure. On the ground floor there were 250 bathhouses plus a recreation room with skating, bowling, pool, Ping-Pong, and shuffleboard. Upstairs there was a large dance hall where people could learn the new two-step and the Boston dip. During the swing era, many big-name bands serenaded dancers during the resort season. The building was replaced by Lighthouse Condominiums.

The Spring Lake public beach at one time had a structure called Lakeside Pavilion. Located at the north end of Lake Avenue, the pavilion offered visitors a place to park their tin lizzies, change clothes, and buy sandwiches and drinks. The public beach still offers a sandy spot for sunning or swimming in Spring Lake, but the pavilion is long since gone.

Originally the site of the North Shore Cabana Club, developed by Harold Warm in the 1920s, the 20-acre lakefront property now known as North Shore Park was purchased from Warm and dedicated in 1941. The County Road Commission, then in charge of parks, spent $7,854 for a parking lot, restrooms, a concession/ bathhouse, and a pavilion. The park, which includes 745 feet on Lake Michigan, remains a popular spot today and looks little different than it did in the postcard view of 60 years ago.

A popular destination for tourists was the elegant Highland Park Hotel, where some families made return visits for generations. Built around 1890, the two-story frame hotel featured 36 rooms in the main lodge and 15 more in the 1906 annex. Porches on both levels extended the full length of the building, and the roof was topped by a dome. Fire destroyed the hotel on the night of December 20, 1967, but the annex survived and today is a privately owned cottage.

As early as 1857, Bridget Brady operated a boardinghouse at the northeast corner of Savidge and Division Streets in Spring Lake, the building at the far left of the postcard picture. Two years later, Robert Clydesdell was the owner. Subsequent owners included Lewis Barnum, Walter Sinclair, and Sylvester Rideout in 1879. John Castle was proprietor of the Rideout Hotel in 1893. For awhile, the hotel also was called the Central House. Today Plantenga Cleaners occupies the site.

Constructed in the late 1800s on Spring Lake, Prospect Point Manor was one of many resorts that once was a fruit orchard. In the 1940s, an advertisement read, "Modern Lodge and private Hotel Cottages. Accommodations for 150 guests. Unusual meals . . . private beach . . . golf and tennis nearby . . . shuffleboard . . . motion pictures . . . water sports . . . organized entertainment. Midnight snacks. Select clientele." Condominiums replaced the resort after fire destroyed it in 1971.

In 1926, Frank and Florence Reghel purchased the 14-unit Oval Inn, located on Harbor Drive across the street from the state park in Grand Haven. The Reghels added the nearby Grand Haven Apartments and the Miami Apartments for a total of 40 rooms and four apartments. Food service was offered from 9:00 a.m. to midnight. The Reghels sold their interest in the property in 1955. In 1997, the building was sold again, remodeled extensively, and reopened by Mike Weavers under the name Blue Water Inn.

Frank and Florence Reghel owned the frame, three-story Miami Apartments at 27 Prospect Street. The ground floor of the Miami Apartments was used as a three-stall garage, with two more garages attached to the east side of the complex. The apartments were located on the two upper stories. The Reghels resided in one of them. The two-stall garage to the east was replaced by a three-story addition, while the other garages were removed and converted to apartments.

An 1897 issue of *Headlight Flashes* publicized Strawberry Point, which was adjacent to Spring Lake Beach at the north end of Lake Street and extended eastward along the lake's shoreline. Undoubtedly "luscious wild strawberries" once grew in the area, but the subdivision of small lots was called Spring Lake Beach, and Strawberry Point referred to the land along Spring Lake just to the east. Many of the early cottages have been razed, moved, or substantially remodeled.

In the 1950s, Elmer C. Sicard resided at 213 Rex Street in Spring Lake. He owned and managed a two-unit log structure just to his south at 201–203 Rex Street, which he rented as Sicard's Apartment Log Cabins. Today the home on the corner is well hidden by greenery. Sicard advertised that his cabins had a "Private Beach—Quiet, Restful Cabins for your vacation pleasure." Access to the lake was a short one-block walk north.

CHAPTER 2

ESTATES, HOMES, AND COTTAGES

Jay Johnston, who joined Johnston Boiler Company in Ferrysburg in 1897 as president, lived in this house on Sheldon Road in Grand Haven. After he died in 1964, Edward and Lynn Kinkema took ownership and continue to reside there. Edward was a building contractor. The historic photograph was taken by Grand Haven photographer Bill Moser at the height of the severe winter of 1935–1936.

Dentist Enoch P. Cummings built this majestic Queen Anne–style three-story home in 1892. It had four bedrooms on the second floor, a ballroom and billiard room on the third, and three fireplaces. A carriage house, built near the west edge of the lot, provided living quarters for servants and a gardener and served also as a barn for horses, a cow, chickens, and guinea pigs. Scott Bekins purchased the home in 2000 and restored it as nearly as possible to its original design.

In 1899, Nathaniel and Esther Robbins built a home at 20 South Fifth Street for $25,000, an extravagant sum in those days. Designed in the classical revival style, the home's 8,500 square feet included an entry hall, an open stairway, spacious "public" rooms, eight bedrooms, seven baths, and a ballroom on the third floor. Later owners Laura and Ed Grafton completely refinished it in 1994. In 2002, William Swano purchased the property as office space for Pacor Home Mortgage Company.

In 1871, Hunter Savidge built a majestic frame home as the family residence in Spring Lake. In the estate's early years, cows and pigs grazed in the yard. Catherine and William Loutit made their home here in 1948. After Catherine's death in 1962, the property went to her nephew Sandy Luce. The house was razed in 1967 and platted for a subdivision. The brick gates, erected in 1871 to mark the entrance to the estate, still stand at the corners of Liberty and Cutler Streets.

In 1920, Nathaniel and Esther Robbins constructed a two-story brick home in Spring Lake as a summer home for their son Hunter and his wife. Gary and Victoria Ver Plank purchased the home from Hunter's second wife, Clara Belle, in 1977. The Ver Planks winterized the house and made it a year-round residence. Little of the exterior has changed over the years. The home was built near the site of Spring Lake House, a popular resort with "magnetic waters," which burned down in 1916.

Lake Avenue was laid out through the wooded dunes in 1873, the first road to go from downtown Grand Haven to the Lake Michigan shoreline. Robert and Martha Duncan owned considerable acreage, including the area where Lake Avenue turns west. They built two homes on the corner and resided in the nearer one. A bequest from the Duncans gave Grand Haven 50 acres of forested land across the street from their home, an area now known as Duncan Park.

John and Catherine Powell's two-story frame home was located at 215 North Seventh Street. He owned a meat market at 207 North Seventh Street. John, a native of the Netherlands, lived from 1837 to 1913. Today the site serves as a parking lot for the adjacent office building.

The first cottage in Highland Park was completed in 1887. Within 20 years, 107 cottages were nestled in the dunes. The frame walls lacked insulation, exposing residents to chilling drafts once the warm breezes of August had departed. Because so many of the cottages were built on the sides of steep dunes and in ravines, wooden stairways and boardwalks were constructed. The cottage pictured in the postcard has changed over the years but has retained its original outline.

HIGHLAND PARK DRIVE, GRAND HAVEN, MICH.

Known now as the Anthony House, this three-story frame structure in Highland Park was built prior to 1920. An extensive deck has been added and the exterior color is different, but the house remains essentially the same as it looked in the 1923 postcard view. Even the masonry retaining wall still stands.

The Herwyn Inn originally was a boardinghouse that served home-cooked meals prepared in a small, hot kitchen. Owner Jane Herwyn met her husband, Ed Peters, in Highland Park. Peters had formerly owned and managed the concessions at the pavilion, later known as the Bil-Mar Restaurant. The inn was passed down and restored by Randy Smith, who then sold it to Claudia Kerr. Its basic structure has been altered very little during the intervening years, and the cottage remains in use today.

In 1927, Anthony Warm constructed a log cabin about a half-mile south of today's North Beach Park. The four-room log cabin remained in place until 1998. Also in 1927, Warm's son Harold built a more substantial two-story Tudor-style home closer to the beach. Harold and his partner distributed a brochure to promote development of the north shore. The Depression slowed its growth but did not stop it. Today the north shore dunes are lined with homes except for the Kitchel-Lundquist Dunes Preserve.

The Thum family had a summer residence on the north side of Spring Lake in the late 19th century. Their boathouse was a story-and-a-half structure with a lookout tower. The Thum brothers perfected and produced Tanglefoot Sticky Fly Paper in Grand Rapids. Spring Lake village took title to the Thum property in 1927 through a bequest, and in 1931, the Spring Lake Yacht Club obtained a long-term lease on the property. Yacht club members built new quarters after high water destroyed the Thum boathouse in 1952.

CHAPTER 3

Travel by Train, Boat, and Car

In the first quarter of the 20th century, the interurban provided a convenient and inexpensive mode of travel between Grand Rapids, Fruitport, Spring Lake, and Grand Haven. A bridge carried the interurban cars across the Grand River from Grand Haven to Spring Lake and they continued from Rix Robinson Park at the southern foot of today's bascule bridge to the present location of the Holiday Inn. From there, the tracks continued eastward and merged with Savidge Street, then known as State Street, as seen in the postcard view.

The Grand Trunk Railway depot opened to train travelers in 1870. An attached warehouse was gone by 1912. Another warehouse, constructed in 1878, lined the banks of the Grand River but was razed in 1958, and the land was purchased by Grand Haven. The depot was occupied by the Tri-Cities Historical Museum in 1972. In 1958—100 years after the line reached Grand Haven—the last passenger train left the depot. Freight trains continued to operate until 1966. The historic picture was taken in 1957.

The train station on Jackson Street, shown in the postcard view, was built in 1870 for the Chicago and West Michigan Railway. It burned down in 1926. Its replacement, a brick structure, was erected the following year and was used by Pere Marquette Railway passengers headed north or south. When passenger service ended in 1971, the building stood unused for many years. In 1997, dentists Walt Weber and Kennard Creason converted it to office and professional space. They restored it to its earlier look.

Around 1912, the Spring Lake interurban station opened at 123 West Savidge Street. After the Grand Rapids, Grand Haven and Muskegon Railway Company terminated interurban service in the mid-1920s, the depot housed a variety of businesses, including the Grain Station, a health food outlet. The building was moved to Coopersville on August 8, 1990, to make room for FMB Lumberman's Bank, which had purchased the property. Huntington Bank eventually took over the site.

CITY SLIP AND DEWEY HILL, GRAND HAVEN, MICH.

Dewey Hill, once a moving sand dune, now is covered with grass, and the fishing shanties that sat at its foot have been replaced by the world's largest musical fountain. The open area, known as William M. Ferry Landing, is the site of a six-foot brass sundial and the expansive Brass River display and is designed to show the geographic placement of the Grand River. The tower on the right served as a ticket office for the Crosby Line steamships.

The first bridge to cross the Grand River between Grand Haven and Spring Lake was built in 1866. Sawdust Road, as it was called because of the many sawmills, continued from the site of Rix Robinson Park northward across the river to the site of today's Holiday Inn. A track was added in 1902 to extend the interurban line to Grand Haven. In 1924, a $250,000 bridge, shown in the postcard, was built west of the first one. The current drawbridge, dedicated in 1955, replaced the swing bridge.

A smaller bridge was needed to span the South Channel of the Grand River. An earlier one, built about the same time as the bascule bridge, was replaced by today's structure when U.S. Route 31 was improved and rerouted in the mid-1950s.

The current bridge that spans Smith's Bayou in Spring Lake Township was built in 1972. The first bridge was replaced by the post-and-beam span shown in the postcard, where several boys stand on the railing ready to jump into the water. The bayou was named for Hezekiah Smith, a freed slave from Kentucky. Smith settled in the area and raised peaches and apples. After his departure, marl was discovered and excavated for use as a fertilizer. Excavation helped enlarge the bayou.

The east–west highway through Spring Lake originally was named State Street. It assumed its new name in honor of William Savidge, who died in 1916. Also serving as a state highway, Savidge Street is designated Michigan Route 104. Seventy years ago, Savidge Street was a quiet, tree-lined, two-lane road. As this view to the west shows, today it is jammed with cars most of the time, especially in the summer.

The postcard view looking east along Savidge Street in Spring Lake village reveals the willow trees that once lined its edges, earning it the nickname Willow Drive. Thomas Savidge planted them in the early 1900s. The later view looking east shows how a quiet, two-lane road has been transformed into a broad highway, now lined with gasoline stations, strip malls, and shops. The last willow tree was removed about 10 years ago.

During the 1950s, the Fireside Inn was the name of a restaurant in the stone and frame building near the northeast corner of Lakeshore Drive and Hayes Street in Grand Haven Township. A two-story wing was added later, and the building was converted to an apartment complex.

Before the cabins pictured here were converted to apartments, they made up Lakeview Court, a motel for highway travelers. It opened in the mid-1930s, when Pine Street in Ferrysburg was designated U.S. Route 31. Although U.S. Route 31 was rerouted in the mid-1950s, Lakeview Motel was still attracting travelers as late as 1971. Dexter Munro was the owner. The complex is located at 501 Pine Street.

Chapter 4

Churches, Schools, and Libraries

In 1866, St. Mary's Catholic Church was built at 208 North Division Street in Spring Lake on land donated by Hunter Savidge. The church, which seated 50 worshipers, is hidden by trees in the postcard picture. In 1882, 35 families, tired of the journey into Grand Haven to worship, purchased a lot just north of St. Mary's and began construction of the building with the steeple. They called themselves the Holland Christian Reformed Church.

After its founding in 1835, the Grand Haven Presbyterian Church met at a building on Second Street. In 1855, church leaders laid a cornerstone for a meetinghouse on Washington Street. In 1872, they purchased land at the southeast corner of Franklin and Fifth Streets, and 13 years later, the church on Washington Street was moved to the new site. Ground was broken for a new sanctuary in 1954, and two years later, the earlier church was razed.

About 20 Catholic families in Grand Haven formally organized St. Patrick's Church in 1867. Among the first pastors to serve St. Patrick's was the Reverend T. J. Murphy, who oversaw construction of the first church in Grand Haven in 1872 and 1873. It is seen in the postcard view. The church now is located at 920 Fulton Street, opposite its earlier site. The house to the left of the original church served as a residence for the priests.

The Second Reformed Church of Grand Haven began on November 22, 1871, when 20 families separated from their mother church. Their first church was built at 600 Washington Street and dedicated on November 26, 1872. That building was destroyed by fire on March 9, 1890, and a second church was dedicated on December 10, 1890. The sanctuary was sold to the Seventh-Day Adventists in 1954, but the Reformed congregation continued to use it until it relocated to 1000 Waverly Road three years later.

The First Reformed Church occupied six buildings during its long history, three of which were destroyed by fire at the northeast corner of Washington and Third Streets. One of the fires is dramatically portrayed in the postcard picture. The faith and determination of its congregation made the First Reformed Church the oldest of the Dutch churches in northwest Ottawa County and the oldest organized church in Grand Haven. After the last fire in 1913, the church was rebuilt in the design pictured in the contemporary view.

In 1862, a group of 10 or 12 Methodist-Episcopalians gathered at the home of Elder William Colby and formed a church. When their first church on South Buchanan Street was destroyed by the fire in 1893, a new one was built at 110 East Savidge Street. The church was dissolved about 1920 and the property sold. Farther east, the Presbyterian church is visible in the early-1900s postcard. It was located where Spring Lake District Library opened on April 15, 2003. The house in the foreground still stands.

The first Central School, a three-story brick structure with an impressive bell tower, opened on a high crest on Sixth Street in 1871. When classes began at the new building in 1871, there were 11 teachers in 11 classrooms. The building burned down in 1901. The second Central School, shown in the postcard, also went up in flames in 1963. This building was replaced and became Central Elementary School. Today the Alternative Education program is headquartered here.

In September 1922, a brick high school for grades 9 through 12 opened on Seventh Street, and old Central High was converted to serve kindergarten through eighth grade. When the high school moved to a new site in 1953, the building on Seventh Street was used for awhile as a junior high school and then razed when a new junior high school opened on Griffin Street in 1967. A playground fills the site today.

In 1953, a high school was built on land owned by the school board near the south end of Seventh Street in an area called Green Hill, which was used for sledding and for baseball and football games. The previous high school, a few blocks north on Seventh Street, was used as a junior high school. In 1997, a $32 million high school campus, built for about 2,200 students, opened its doors in Grand Haven Township. The vacated building became Lakeshore Middle School.

Healy C. Akeley built his residence on the corner of Fifth and Columbus Streets in 1881. In 1887, he donated the property to the Akeley School for Girls, which opened the next year with 11 boarding students. It closed in 1928, and seven years later, construction began on a building to house the fire and police departments. When the two departments moved out, several nonprofit groups occupied the space. The Grand Haven Arts Council occupied the ground floor in the fall of 2008.

The brick, two-story Spring Lake Central School was built in 1893 and 1894 on the northeast corner of Buchanan and Exchange Streets, replacing a frame school that burned down in the extensive fire of 1893. Students used outhouses, and the building was heated with wood. The brick structure at 100 Exchange Street lasted until Holmes School opened in 1952 at 426 River Street. Although the former school site now is a vacant lot, the old foundation remains visible just below the surface.

Ferry School, built to serve grades kindergarten through six, opened its doors in September 1913. The five-acre building site, divided into eight lots, was purchased for $1,600 from Henry J. and Lena Bolt, who had a garden and cow pasture. The building was made of brick, and the main entrance faced Pennoyer Avenue. The high school used the grounds for athletics, and it was known as the best-drained field in the state, according to reports. Ferry School has had several additions in the intervening years.

Carnegie Public Library opened at 15 North Third Street in 1914, and it remained the city library until a new one was constructed on Columbus Street in 1967. The Carnegie library was torn down when a new building was erected in 1967 for a bank now known as Fifth Third. The site is used as a parking lot for the bank.

Grand Haven area residents rejoiced in the summer of 2009 when a renovated and enlarged Loutit District Library opened after 18 months in a temporary location. Elizabeth von Oettingen was head librarian when the Carnegie library moved from 315 North Third Street in 1967 to 407 Columbus Street. The new building, then called the Loutit Library, was made possible through a gift from the Loutit Foundation of more than $815,000 in cash and the land on which the library was built.

In 1857, a two-story frame building served as the county courthouse. A more substantial structure was built in 1894 at a cost of $50,000. It was replaced in 1965. Then in the summer of 2009, a fourth county building was constructed. The newest structure emulates the 1894 building in design but is much larger. Grand Haven City Hall and fire department once sat on the southwest corner of Fifth and Washington Streets. The 1894 building is visible behind their building.

In 1933 and 1934, the Depression-era Works Projects Administration constructed the brick building that houses city hall in the 500 block of Washington Street. Before it was built, the land served as a campus for Akeley Institute, which closed in 1928. The land was purchased by the city in 1933, and two years later, the current city hall opened. The city hall was an adaptation of the Dutch Colonial Revival style. The first city hall on the southwest corner of Washington and Fifth Streets had opened in 1878.

George and Christiana Hubbard were owners of a two-story frame house that stood at 114 South Fifth Street. In 1919, the residence became the area's first hospital, made possible through the generosity of William Hatton. Named the Elizabeth Hatton Memorial Hospital in honor of his deceased wife, it offered 18 beds. Patients had to walk upstairs to the operating room. Hospital services were moved to 1309 Sheldon Road in 1939. The lot subsequently became the site of the Presbyterian church Sunday school.

A brick hospital opened on Sheldon Road in 1939. The two-and-a-half-story building had a capacity of 47 beds and a staff of 10 physicians. The first floor was for medical-surgical patients, and the second floor was for obstetrics, surgeries, and deliveries. In 1953, an obstetrics wing was added to the west. Other substantial additions over the years included a three-story ambulatory care center, completed in 2001 at a cost of $10 million. The care center is attached to the original brick structure.

CHAPTER 5

PUBLIC AND PRIVATE PLACES

Two years after leaving the port of Grand Haven, the Coast Guard cutter *Escanaba* went down in the North Atlantic Ocean in June 1943, taking 101 crew members with it and leaving only two survivors. Through the efforts of many local residents, the *Escanaba*'s 60-foot mast, rigging, and life raft were placed in the former Kelly Park. The area, originally part of Government Basin, was filled in to form a landing for the cutter in 1932. It was renamed Escanaba Park on May 30, 1944.

In the 19th century, Central Park served as Grand Haven's municipal cemetery. In 1883, the city council voted to relocate the bodies to Lake Forest Cemetery on Lake Avenue. The city park board, the Grand Haven Woman's Club, and the Garden Club sodded the park, planted shrubs, and paved walkways. The fountain in the center of the park originally graced the grounds of Sheldon's Magnetic Springs. Today the park provides a refuge for strollers and is an ideal space for special events.

Lake Forest Cemetery on Lake Avenue was barely 20 years old when this 1912 postcard was mailed from Grand Haven to Milwaukee. The original, ornate wrought-iron entrance has been replaced. Points of special interest include grave sites of many prominent citizens, memorials for those who participated in various wars, and the more recently added Sunken Gardens and Babyland. Lake Avenue was not paved at the time of the postcard, but a concrete sidewalk extended at least this far and into the cemetery.

In the late 1800s, John Mulligan settled with his family on land east of Five Mile Hill. During World War II, a Civilian Conservation Corps camp, constructed here in 1938, was used as a Coast Guard training camp. Later known as Mulligan's Hollow, in 1973 the site became a city park that included a picnic area and recreational activities. The YMCA moved from the armory on Second Street to this site in 1975. Volunteers created Imagination Station around 1991, and the ski lodge was erected about 2005.

In 1913, Robert Duncan's widow, Martha, deeded to Grand Haven this forested acreage with the restriction that it remain in its natural state for the benefit of the community. It was known thereafter as Duncan Park. Robert Duncan, who was mayor of Grand Haven from 1868 to 1869, arrived here in 1851 and opened a law practice. The park is located in the 1500 block of Sheldon Road. The stone walls at the entrance were rebuilt around 2001.

Spring Lake obtained this land at the south end of School Street from the Cutler and Savidge Lumber Company when it left the area. It was used as a landfill until 1973. The village constructed a new public works building on the same site in 1976. In 1982, the area west of the building was converted to Mill Point Park. The four-acre site along 1,315 feet of shoreline offers boat-launching pads, restrooms, picnic areas, an observation deck, and parking.

In 1902, the Grand Rapids, Grand Haven, and Muskegon Electric Interurban Company built Pomona Pavilion on the shores of Spring Lake in Fruitport. Boaters could moor at the building and join the fun, which included many big band dances. When it burned down on January 24, 1963, Alfred Lilly and his brother-in-law Jimmy Simms were owners. They had taken possession the previous December 24th and had held just one dance, a New Year's Eve gala. Today the site is a public park.

In 1905, Company F built the armory at 15 South Second Street to be used for meetings and drills. Company F saw action in both World War I and World War II. The armory gymnasium was used for dances, stage shows, and high school basketball games, and from 1963 to 1976, it housed the YMCA. A shrinking budget forced the armory to shut down in 1995. In 2004, the armory was remodeled into residential and office space, and Bea's Medical Spa opened on the first floor.

Spring Lake Country Club, founded in 1911 when shareholders purchased the Benjamin Soule farm for $6,000, started with a nine-hole golf course. The farmhouse was converted to a clubhouse and the barn to a men's locker room. At first, golfers reached the club on the interurban or by foot. As membership grew, the course was expanded to 18 holes. In 1925, the club built the Spanish-style clubhouse seen today. Despite many improvements, it looks essentially as it did at the time the clubhouse was built.

Sawmill owner John W. Hopkins built his residence on Third Street prior to 1864. After his death, Stephen Munroe bought the property. The home, located next to the Cutler house at Third and Washington Streets, was damaged in the fire of 1889. Years later, Col. George Olson moved the house to 301 Sherman Avenue. In 1928, the Elks Club constructed on the Third Street site a masonry building with a tile roof. Little has changed on the exterior of the building since its construction.

CHAPTER 6

COMMERCIAL AND MANUFACTURING SITES

Christmas 1958 was a bustling time in downtown Grand Haven. Shoppers did not hesitate to pull into the metered parking spaces. Most of the businesses flourishing then have since left the scene. Grand Haven State Bank, the structure with the Ionic columns at the far right, is now an office building. Next door, the Robinhood Theater was razed, and the site is now a small park. Reichardt's, across the street, eventually shut its doors, and its neighbor Wheeler's Rexall Drug Store closed in 1970.

Dewey Hill was a favorite place for photographers to get bird's-eye views of downtown Grand Haven. A few of the buildings seen in the early-1900s picture remain in use today, including Kirby's Grill, with its third floor removed, and the Story and Clark Piano Company, now a retail mall. The old and new courthouses can be identified by their distinctive cupolas. Central School is prominent at right center. The passenger steamer *Nyack* is moored near the Crosby ticket office.

These scenes, also taken from Dewey Hill, provide a panoramic view of Grand Haven Harbor at one of its many busy times. Two large ferryboats are lined up near the railroad tracks and grain elevator to pick up loads for the trip across Lake Michigan. The north end of the Story and Clark Piano Factory can be seen through the smoke, and South Channel cuts eastward at the far left. The grain elevator burned down in 1914.

The postcard view, taken from the foot of Washington Street, features Nat Robbins's office in the lower right corner. It is now headquarters for the Tri-Cities Chamber of Commerce. The third floor of the Gildner Hotel, across the street, was removed in 1965. Today Kirby's Grill occupies the two remaining floors. At various times, the hotel has been known as the Ferry, the Gildner, and the Schuler. The interurban ran down Washington Street and along Harbor Drive to the waterfront.

In 1872, Grand Haven's post office was erected on the corner of First and Washington Streets, a structure that today houses the Rosebud Restaurant. The post office remained in this building until a new one was built in 1905 two blocks east. By 1907, James Van Wessem's ice-cream parlor offered sodas and sundaes for a nickel. The frame buildings on the opposite corner have disappeared, but the three-story brick structure, where Pfaff's Hardware Store was located, today is the home of Michigan Rag Company.

This view, looking west along Washington Street toward Dewey Hill, is much greener today than it was around 1910. Many of the familiar shops on both sides of Washington Street now are hidden by trees. In the postcard view, the post office dominated the corner of Washington and Third Streets, now occupied by Fifth Third Bank. At the far end of Washington Street is Dewey Hill, now looking more like a grass-covered mound than a sand dune. The main street was paved with brick in 1910.

Grand Haven businessman Willard C. Sheldon found mineral water at the corner of Washington and Third Streets in 1871. He promptly erected a resort with the look of a sanitarium that attracted visitors who wished to "take the waters." The two-story main building was 100 feet long and 50 feet wide. The grounds were beautifully landscaped, and activities included croquet, archery, and lawn bowling. In 1905, the resort was razed and a post office was built in its place. Today the site is home to Fifth Third Bank.

Peoples Bank was organized in the winter of 1910 and occupied space at 220 Washington Street while its new office building was being completed that year at 300 Washington Street. Grand Haven's only armed bank robbery occurred here in 1933. In 1977, the bank razed adjacent buildings to make room for expansion and parking. Three years later, the original bank building was expanded and completely remodeled, concealing the original structure. Chase Bank is the current owner.

Gerrit Bottje and Son Hardware Store moved into this building when John and Gerrit Juistema completed its construction in 1887. In 1918, Claude Beukema bought the building and business, which he named Beukema and Company Hardware. Beukema sold the building in 1930, and for a time it was vacant until the Food Center Grocery opened. It was followed by the Michigan Liquor Control Commission Store and then a variety of small shops. Today it is occupied by Running Circles, which offers athletic footwear and accessories.

The first occupant at 204 Washington Street was Daniel Gale's drugstore in 1871. An 1894 map of Grand Haven identified the store as dealing in groceries and crockery. The drugstore was destroyed in the 1889 fire, the westernmost building to be affected by the blaze. Gale's business was followed by Charles Reghel's saloon, which opened about 1902, and then the Colonial Café, which was owned and operated by Mrs. L. C. Pennoyer, as shown in the interior scene. Today Ceramic Café occupies the space.

Derk Baker and his brother Jeltz erected a sawmill on the south bank of the South Channel in 1871. When the supply of trees declined, Derk chose to become a lumber dealer, supplying lumber, lath, shingles, and siding to area builders. Derk's son John took over the company in 1907 and in 1912 relocated it to its present site at 720 Pennoyer Avenue. Baker Lumber remains a family business today. The historic picture, taken from the back of the building, is dated 1912. (Historic image, Bruce Baker.)

In the 1940s, this building at the corner of Seventh and Elliott Streets housed the Peerless Glove Company, which earlier had been located at 13 South Second Street. Arthur W. Elliott and Abraham Reenders were the owners. Peerless made heavy-duty work gloves. Laughead Piano Company located here sometime after 1957, moving from its 122 Washington Street address. Today the building is a residential condominium. The building faces Elliott Street.

In 1868, Clark Albee moved his leather company to a new building at the north end of Beechtree Street. Its origins date to 1838, when Horace Sheldon started a tannery near downtown Grand Haven. Known as Grand Haven Leather Company in 1885, it was purchased by Eagle Tanning Works in 1901. Beginning in 1916, it was named Eagle Ottawa Leather Company. The business closed permanently in 2007. The smoke visible in the 1913 postcard view attests to its productivity at that time.

City Hall, Spring Lake, Mich.

The first Spring Lake Village Hall was built at the corner of Savidge and Buchanan Streets in 1872. In 1937, the Work Projects Administration erected a new building, which is still in use. The police and fire departments had offices in this building, and the library was also located there. The village council convened in a chamber on the second floor until Barber School was moved and remodeled. The building was renovated and enlarged in June 2005 at a cost of $877,000.

This corner, in Spring Lake, once was the site of Andrew Fall's grocery store. In 1915, William Spencer and John Singerland bought the grocery business. Julia Falls sold the building in 1923 to Leon Campbell for a drugstore. Clarence Eshleman, who had worked for Campbell since 1930, purchased the business in 1948, and 16 years later, his son Jon joined as partner. About 1996, Rite-Aid took over the corner but eventually moved into a new building farther east on Savidge. Love Inc. now occupies the site.